GROUNDCOVER
SERIES

This book is dedicated to the memory of Indru Prito Shahani.

Acknowledgements

I would like to thank a number of people who have helped me during
the preparation of this book:

First and foremost my wife Delyth and family for their continued
encouragement and support.

Special thanks go to Helen Webb at Kelmscott Manor; the staff of Eton College;
Clare Murphy and Annie Heron at Hampton Court Palace; Richard Pailthorpe
at Syon Park; Malcolm Godfrey at The Old Royal Naval College; the staff of the
Globe Theatre; The National Trust; English Heritage.

I particularly wish to thank all the staff at Jarrold Publishing
for their help and advice.

GERAINT TELLEM

The quotes on the following pages are reproduced by kind permission of the parties shown:
p82 from *Waterloo Sunset* by Ray Davies © 1967 Davray Music Ltd and Carlin Music Corp – All Rights Reserved
p100 from *London River* by Gavin Weightman, Collins & Brown, 1990
p109 from a BBC News broadcast by Nick Higham, 2000
p116 from *The River's Tale* by Rudyard Kipling, from *Rudyard Kipling: The Complete Verse*, Kyle Cathie Ltd, 1990,
by permisssion of A.P. Watt Ltd on behalf of The Natonal Trust for Places of Historical Interest or Natural Beauty

Every effort has been made to secure permission from copyright owners to use the extracts featured in this book.
Any subsequent correspondence should be sent to Jarrold Publishing,
Healey House, Dene Road, Andover, Hampshire, SP10 2AA.

Front cover picture: Westminster Bridge and the Houses of Parliament
Back cover picture: The Thames, looking east from Waterloo Bridge

Published by: Jarrold Publishing,
Healey House, Dene Road, Andover,
Hampshire, SP10 2AA.
Sales: 01264 409206
Enquiries: 01264 409200
Fax: 01264 334110
e-mail: heritagesales@jarrold.com
website: www.britguides.com

Publication in this form © copyright Jarrold
Publishing, 2003.
Text written and researched by John McIlwain.
The author has asserted his moral rights.
Designed by Tim Noel-Johnson.
Front cover designed by John Buckley.
Map by Tim Noel-Johnson.

All photographs by Geraint Tellem.
All photographs © copyright Geraint Tellem and
Jarrold Publishing.

ISBN 0 7117 2411 3

Printed in Belgium.

1/03

PUBLISHER'S NOTE
Variant and archaic spellings have been retained
in quoted material, while the modern spellings
of place names have been used in headings.
The inclusion of a photograph in this book
does not necessarily imply public access to the
place or building illustrated.

THE THAMES

JARROLD
publishing

London Eye from Victoria Embankment

THE THAMES

GERAINT TELLEM

GROUNDCOVER
SERIES

Thames Barrier

Contents

Introduction

Deep in rural Gloucestershire, in the corner of a quiet meadow known as Trewsbury Mead, the Thames, Britain's longest river, begins its 215-mile (350-km) journey to the North Sea. However, this official source, marked by a stone monument, is dry for much of the year. Rather, the river emerges gradually over the next few miles, the starting point depending on the amount of rainfall. The Thames is essentially a lowland river with a rich diversity of wildlife, flowing for much of its length through a gentle landscape of woods, meadows and grassland.

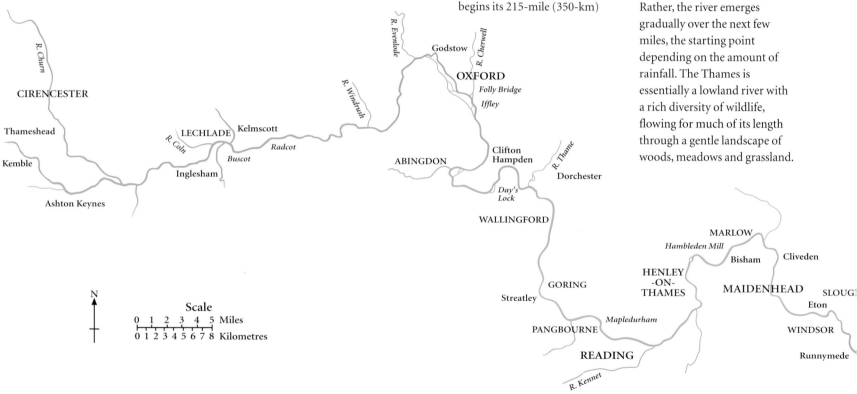

R. Churn

CIRENCESTER

Thameshead

Kemble

Ashton Keynes

R. Coln

LECHLADE

Kelmscott

Inglesham

Buscot

Radcot

R. Windrush

R. Evenlode

Godstow

R. Cherwell

OXFORD

Folly Bridge

Iffley

ABINGDON

Clifton Hampden

R. Thame

Dorchester

Day's Lock

WALLINGFORD

MARLOW

Hambleden Mill

Bisham

Cliveden

GORING

HENLEY -ON- THAMES

MAIDENHEAD

SLOUGH

Streatley

Mapledurham

Eton

PANGBOURNE

WINDSOR

READING

Runnymede

R. Kennet

N

Scale
0 1 2 3 4 5 Miles
0 1 2 3 4 5 6 7 8 Kilometres

John Burns once described The Thames as 'liquid history'. Since neolithic times the river has had a tradition of farming, milling, fishing and trade. As its importance increased, castles and forts were built along the Thames to defend against attack, and following the Roman invasion of AD 43, the port of London (the Romans called it *Londinium*) grew up. Many key historical figures have lived on or near the Thames, and along its banks, country houses, abbeys, picturesque towns and villages, watermills and palaces are found.

Boats have travelled the river as far up as Oxford since the 12th century, but it wasn't until the end of the 17th century that pound locks were introduced, making navigation possible for 191 miles (307 km) up to Lechlade. These locks, together with the growth of an interlinking canal system, turned the Thames into one of the country's major waterways. Although rail and road put an end to commercial river transport, there are still important links with maritime trade, centred around the docks at Tilbury and Sheerness.

The mid-19th century saw an explosion of interest in the Thames as a source of leisure activity; water-bound sports such as boating, angling, canoeing, punting and rowing have been strongly associated with the river ever since.

This book takes a leisurely photographic journey along the Thames and highlights some of its many and varied features – the tranquil upper reaches, the splendour of Windsor Castle and Hampton Court Palace, the teeming activity of London and the broad expanse of the estuary. There were photographic opportunities throughout its length but, for me, the river was at its best one morning in early summer, the rising sun reflected on mist-laden water in a remote Oxfordshire meadow, near where the story of the Thames begins.

GERAINT TELLEM, August 2002

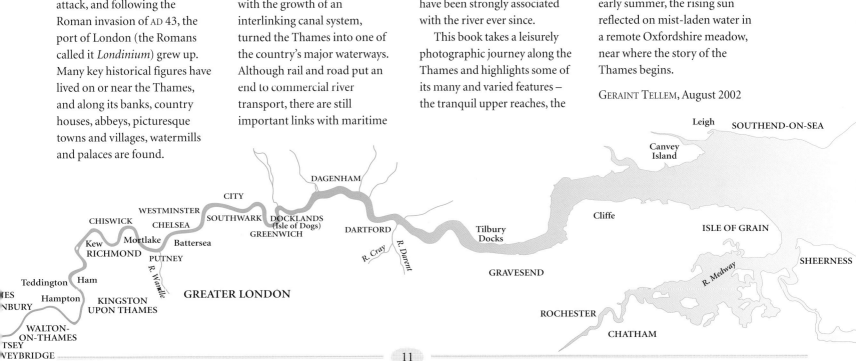

THAMESHEAD
TREWSBURY MEAD

The Thames, the longest river in England, has its origin in the Cotswold Hills. Here in Trewsbury Mead, just off the Fosse Way near Kemble, a stone beneath an ash tree marks where water first breaks the surface (in a wet winter, at least). This modest beginning speaks little of the greatness to come downstream.

THE CONSERVATORS OF THE RIVER THAMES
1857 – 1974
THIS STONE WAS PLACED HERE TO MARK THE
SOURCE OF THE RIVER THAMES

NEAR LYD WELL

But Cotswold, be this spoke to th'only praise of thee,
That thou of all the rest, the chosen soil shouldst be,
Dame Isis to bring forth (the mother of the Thames).
With whose delicious brooks, by whose immortal streams
Her greatness is begun.

MICHAEL DRAYTON
Polyolbion

ASHTON KEYNES

Along the shore of silver streaming Themmes,
Whose rutty Bancke, the which his river hemmes,
Was paynted all with variable flowers,
And all the meades adorned with daintie gemmes,
Fit to decke maydens bowres,
And crowne their Paramours,
Against the Brydale day, which is not long:
Sweet Themmes runne softly, till I end my Song.

EDMUND SPENSER
Prothalamion

INGLESHAM

The tiny 13th-century church of St John the Baptist, on the river bank at Inglesham, was sensitively restored in 1888–9 by the Society for the Protection of Ancient Buildings, under the supervision of William Morris of nearby Kelmscott (see pages 26–27).

St John the Baptist Church, Inglesham

NEAR LECHLADE

'The Mole was bewitched, entranced, fascinated. By the side of the river he trotted as one trots, when very small, by the side of a man who holds one spellbound by exciting stories; and when, tired at last, he sat on the bank, while the river still chattered on to him, a babbling procession of the best stories in the world, sent from the heart of the earth to be told at last to the insatiable sea.'

KENNETH GRAHAME
The Wind in the Willows

LECHLADE

Halfpenny (or Town) Bridge at Lechlade marks where navigation starts on the Thames, the first of over 100 bridges to cross the navigable section. A halfpenny pedestrian toll, imposed when the bridge replaced a ferry in 1792, was lifted after the locals revolted in 1839. The toll house still survives.

CHURCH OF ST LAWRENCE
LECHLADE

Silence and Twilight, unbeloved of men,
Creep hand in hand from yon obscurest glen.
They breathe their spells towards the departing day,
Encompassing the earth, air, stars and sea;
Light, sound, and motion own the potent sway,
Responding to the charm with its own mystery.
The winds are still, or the dry church-tower grass
Knows not their gentle motions as they pass.

PERCY BYSSHE SHELLEY
Stanzas in A Summer Evening Churchyard, Lechlade, Gloucestershire

NEAR LECHLADE

Since 1066 when William the Conqueror's army crossed the Thames at Wallingford, fortifications have been built along the river. Less elegant than William's Norman castles were the 5,000 or so 'pill-boxes' (gun posts) built in 1939–40 across the south of England from Chatham to Bristol against Hitler's threatened invasion.

OLD FATHER THAMES
LECHLADE

Below Lechlade is St John's Lock, the first on the Thames. Near the lock is Old Father Thames, a sculpture by Rafaelle Monti created from Portland cement for the Great Exhibition of 1851. Before 1974, it stood at the source of the Thames, Trewsbury Mead.

BUSCOT HOUSE

The house, built by Edward Townsend in the Adam style *c.*1780, is owned by The National Trust. Within is the Faringdon collection of paintings by English and European masters. Special to Buscot is the Briar Rose series of painted panels representing the story of the Sleeping Beauty, brought to life by the famous Pre-Raphaelite, Sir Edward Burne-Jones.

KELMSCOTT MANOR

'Heaven on earth … An old stone Elizabeth house, and such a garden! Close down by the river, a boathouse. All things handy.'

WILLIAM MORRIS, founder of the Arts and Crafts movement, on discovering Kelmscott, which he owned from 1871 until his death in 1896.

MORRIS'S BEDROOM

'[Kelmscott] has come to be with me the type of the pleasant places of the earth … As others love the race through their lovers or their children, so I love the earth through that small space of it.'

WILLIAM MORRIS

Cart wheels, Kelmscott

RADCOT BRIDGE

Radcot Bridge has claims to being the oldest on the Thames, having been built in the 14th century. Its piers may be far older still, and Saxon manuscripts record a stone bridge here.

GODSTOW

By the Thames on the fringes of Oxford are the ruins of the 12th-century Godstow nunnery, dissolved by Henry VIII in 1539 and burnt down in the Civil War (1645). The famous Trout Inn, pictured overleaf, was once its guesthouse. Godstow Lock was built in 1790 using prisoners from Oxford Jail.

THE TROUT INN
GODSTOW

On 4 July 1862 the Revd Charles Dodgson, a
mathematics lecturer of Christ Church College,
accompanied the three daughters of Dr Liddell, Dean
of Christ Church, on a rowing boat trip upstream to
Godstow for a picnic. On the way he entertained them
with a story, which began 'Alice was beginning to get
very tired of sitting by her sister on the bank and of
having nothing to do'. The classic children's story
Alice's Adventures in Wonderland was born.

TOM TOWER
CHRIST CHURCH, OXFORD

Tom Tower at Christ Church was completed
in its upper half by Sir Christopher Wren. Its
6.5 tonne bell, Great Tom, chimes 101 times each
night at 9.05, curfew time for the college's original
100 students, with one chime added by bequest.

CHRIST CHURCH
OXFORD

Christ Church, Oxford, was
founded in 1524 by Cardinal
Wolsey in Britain's oldest
university city. It is the largest
of all the colleges, providing
Oxford with its cathedral.
Built with money raised
by the dissolution of
St Frideswide's Priory and
other religious houses
elsewhere, it came perilously
close to extinction itself when
Wolsey fell from power.

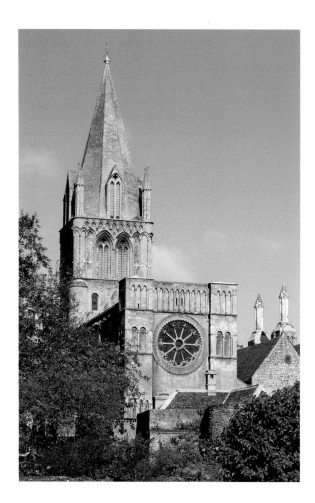

The clever men at Oxford
Know all that there is to be knowed.
But they none of them know one half as much
As intelligent Mr Toad.

KENNETH GRAHAME
The Wind in the Willows

at **FOLLY BRIDGE**

'Between Iffley and Oxford is the most difficult bit of the river I know …. The man who could row a straight course from Oxford to Iffley ought to be able to live comfortably, under one roof, with his wife, his mother-in-law, his eldest sister, and the old servant who was in the family when he was a baby. First the current drives you on to the right bank, and then on to the left, then it takes you out into the middle, turns you round three times, and carries you up-stream again, and always ends by trying to smash you up against a college barge.'

JEROME K. JEROME
Three Men in a Boat

ABINGDON

For a week in July a small
flotilla of skiffs, bearing
official flags and rowed by
liveried watermen, carries out
the 600-year-old ritual of
swan-upping. Between here
and Sunbury, cygnets are
tagged and adult swans
checked for health.
The ceremony dates from
the time when the birds were
the exclusive property of the
Crown and considered a
great delicacy.

Left: Iffley Lock, Oxford

CLIFTON HAMPDEN

'If you stay the night at Clifton [Hampden] you cannot do better than put up at the Barley Mow. It is without exception, I should say, the quaintest, most old-world inn on the river. It stands on the right of the bridge, quite away from the village. Its low-pitched gables and thatched roof and latticed windows give it quite a story-book appearance, while inside it is even still more once-upon-a-timeyfied.'

Jerome K. Jerome
Three Men in a Boat, written, in part, at the Barley Mow.

CLIFTON HAMPDEN

Clifton Hampden's fine brick bridge links Oxfordshire to the north with Berkshire to the south. Despite its Norman appearance, it is Victorian, built in 1864 by the doyen of English cathedral architects, Sir George Gilbert Scott. At one time it was home to Britain's largest colony of house martins. In St Michael's Church nearby, also designed by Scott, is a memorial to Sergeant William Dyke, the man who fired the first shot at the Battle of Waterloo.

DAY'S LOCK

'The mildest tempered people, when on land become violent and bloodthirsty when in a boat. When another boat gets in my way, I feel I want to take an oar and kill all the people in it.'

JEROME K. JEROME
Three Men in a Boat

LITTLE WITTENHAM

Here where the reaper was at work of late,
In this high field's dark corner, where he leaves
His coat, his basket and his earthen cruse,
And in the sun all morning binds the sheaves,
Then here at noon, comes back his stores to use,
Here will I sit and wait
While to my ear from uplands far away
The bleating of the folded flocks is borne,
With distant cries of reapers in the corn –
All the live murmur of a Summer's day.

MATTHEW ARNOLD
High Summer, Oxfordshire

MAPLEDURHAM MILL

Mapledurham is an isolated, almost feudal village by the Thames. At its core is the red-brick manor built in Elizabethan times and still owned by descendants of the Blount family. Nearby is the only working mill left on the River Thames, from the many hundreds that used to exist. After 30 years of disuse, it was restored in the 1970s.

Left: Goring Lock

ST MARGARET'S
MAPLEDURHAM

St Margaret's Church was for many years the subject of royal patronage, not least because one of William IV's illegitimate children was vicar here in the 19th century.

BOATHOUSES
HENLEY-ON-THAMES

Many of Henley's Georgian frontages hide medieval beams within, telling of the town's past as an inland port. These days it is an elegant commuter town, but for a few sparkling days in July, the trend is reversed. At the Henley Royal Regatta, the elite of the rowing world slide, sweating, by as city slickers in boaters and blazers sip champagne in corporate marquees.

HAMBLEDEN MILL
BUCKINGHAMSHIRE

'The village of Hambledon [sometimes spelt Hambleden] is a superb example of what most people imagine an English village to be like. Clustered around the Church and Manor House, the beautifully kept flint-and-brick gabled houses and shops have an atmosphere of peace and contentment which acts as a soothing balm after the turmoil and tumult of a large town.'

FRANK MARTIN
History, People and Places in The Thames Valley

TEMPLE ISLAND, HENLEY-ON-THAMES

The Grecian temple on Temple Island, a mile (2 km) or so downstream of Henley at the north end of the straight stretch of water known as Henley Reach. The island is the starting point for Henley's regatta events.

WINDSOR CASTLE

What was once William the Conqueror's hunting lodge grew to be the largest inhabited castle in the world. The walls are steeped in history. Here King John was besieged in his own halls, Edward III established the Order of the Garter and George IV spent a million pounds on the apartments alone. To escape from the soot and fog of London, Victoria and Albert spent £800,000 turning it from a fortress into a home. In the magnificent St George's Chapel ten former sovereigns are buried.

About, about!
Search Windsor Castle, elves, within and out:
Strew good luck, ouphes, on every sacred room,
That it may stand till the perpetual doom,
In state as wholesome as in state 'tis fit,
Worthy the owner and the owner it.

from *The Merry Wives of Windsor,* first performed by Shakespeare and his company before Queen Elizabeth I at Windsor in 1593.

ETON COLLEGE

Perhaps the most famous school in the world, Eton College was founded by Henry VI in 1440 for 'seventy indigent scholars'. Today the scholars, still in their traditional tail coats, are not so indigent!

Prepositors [monitors] in the feld whan they play, for fyghtyng, rent clothes, blew eyes, or sich other.

Prepositors for yll-kept hedys, unwasshid facys, fowle clothis and sich other.

When any dothe come newe, the master doth enquire fro whens he comyth, what frendys he hath, whether there be any plage.

Educational charters and documents of Eton, 1530

MAGNA CARTA MEMORIAL
RUNNYMEDE

This is the place
Where England's ancient barons, clad in arms,
And stern with conquest, from the tyrant king
(Then rendered tame), did challenge and secure
The charter of thy freedom.

MARK AKENSIDE
Inscription for Runnymede

COMMONWEALTH AIR FORCES MEMORIAL
RUNNYMEDE

This striking memorial on Cooper's Hill, Runnymede, near Windsor, was designed by Sir Edward Maufe, who also designed the Magna Carta Memorial nearby. It contains the names of 20,456 airmen who have no known grave.

HAMPTON COURT PALACE

Cardinal Wolsey's gift to Henry VIII of the huge and beautiful palace he had built by the river at Hampton failed to save him from the charge of high treason when he fell from favour. This magnificent Tudor building, surely one of the finest in Europe, breathes history. Within, the visitor can see sumptuous decor, priceless paintings, exquisite tapestries and superb furniture. Beyond its walls, the gardens alone would repay a day's visit.

HAMPTON COURT PALACE

To thee, my silver-footed Thamesis
Nor more shall I reiterate thy Strand,
Whereon so many stately structures stand:
Nor in the summer's sweeter evenings go
To bathe in thee as thousand others do;
Nor more shall I along thy crystal glide
In barge with boughs and rushes beautified,
With soft, smooth virgins for our chaste disport,
To Richmond, Kingston, and to Hampton Court.

ROBERT HERRICK
Thames

TEDDINGTON LOCK

Teddington is the upper limit of the tidal river, and consequently the river downstream of the locks is under the control of the Port of London Authority. From a room here, the vast flow of water at times of flood is controlled at the push of a button. Even in normal times, between three and four million gallons of water flow over the weirs each day.

HAM HOUSE

'Ham House is a perfect model of the mansion of the last [18th] century, with its shadowy front, its steps and terraces, its marble basins and deep silent court … Everything about it belongs to the time of hoops and periwigs.'

MARY RUSSELL MITFORD
Recollections of a Literary Life

HAM HOUSE

'I have now ranged the best part of Middlesex, a county made rich, pleasant and populous by the neighbourhood of London.'

DANIEL DEFOE
Tour through England and Wales

'All Middlesex is ugly, notwithstanding the millions which it is constantly sucking up from the rest of the kingdom.'

WILLIAM COBBETT
Rural Rides

RICHMOND

These are thy charms fair Richmond, and through these,
The river wafting many a graceful bark,
Glides swiftly onwards like a lovely dream,
Making the scene a paradise.

JAMES THOMSON
Lines on Richmond

SYON HOUSE

Here in the 18th century, the magical abilities of designer Robert Adam and landscaper 'Capability' Brown were brought to bear on an ancient abbey owned by the Dukes of Northumberland. Traditionally renowned for the quality and antiquity of its gardens, Syon House stares at Kew over the river, as if in opposition.

THE ROYAL BOTANIC GARDENS, Kew

Even for those who garden with paving slabs and decking, there
is much to tempt the eyes and nose at Kew. Once a riverside
playground for a royal residence, Kew Palace, the grounds were
developed over the years by Brown, Banks, Paxton and other
horticultural celebrities into a feast of plants and flowers.

'The bargemen were drunk, the poles would scarce reach the
bottom, and in five minutes the rapidity of the current turned the
barge round … The drunkest of the men cried out 'She is gone,
she is lost!' meaning they had lost the management. Lady Browne
fell into an agony, began screaming and praying to Jesus, and
every land and water god and goddess, and I, who expected not
to stop till we should run against Kew Bridge, was contriving how
I should get home.'

HORACE WALPOLE
Letters, 1774

PUTNEY ROWERS

The annual boat race between Oxford and Cambridge begins here at Putney, in west London. The first race took place in 1829, and the event is now a treasured feature of the English sporting calendar.

ALBERT BRIDGE

The Albert Bridge spans the river near the finish of the race for Doggett's Coat and Badge, rowed by young Thames watermen. Founded in 1714, it is one of the oldest sporting events in the world, and pre-dates the bridge by over 150 years.

BATTERSEA

The former Battersea Power Station, with its fluted chimneys and sculptured brickwork, is a fine example of contemporary industrial architecture. It was designed by Sir Giles Gilbert Scott and completed in 1934. Although its use has changed, the elegant shell remains as a cherished part of London's riverside landscape.

VAUXHALL CROSS

The MI6 building at Vauxhall Cross, London, was designed by Terry Farrell. On its opening in 1994 it attracted many unwelcome sobriquets, 'Babylon-on-Thames' and 'Legoland' amongst them. There is no doubt, however, that this powerful symbol of the post-Cold War world adds interest and vitality to London's riverside scene.

WESTMINSTER ABBEY

Perhaps more than any other building in England, the Abbey encapsulates the nation's history. Here were crowned all the sovereigns since William the Conqueror. Here the great and the good of many centuries are buried or commemorated. The striking west front, pictured left, was designed by Sir Christopher Wren and his assistant, Nicholas Hawksmoor.

HOUSES OF PARLIAMENT

Thou stately stream that with the swelling tide
'Gainst London walls incessantly dost beat,
Thou Thames, I say, where barge and boat doth ride,
And snow-white swans do fish for needful meat …

GEORGE TURBERVILLE
Epitaphs, Epigrams, Songs and Sonnets

Charles Dickens wrote on 7 July 1858 of the river
at Westminster, 'the Thames in London is most horrible …
I can certify that the offensive smells, even in that short
whiff, have been of a most head-and-stomach distending
nature'. Sheets soaked in disinfectant were hung from the
windows of Parliament in an effort to keep the stench at bay.

LONDON EYE

London Eye was unquestionably one of the most successful developments of the millennium year. Not only has it attracted millions of visitors to enjoy the superb views of the river and the city, but it has also become an unusual and attractive feature of the riverside landscape.

EMBANKMENT PLACE

Embankment Place (designed in the 1980s by Terry Farrell) stands boldly astride the tracks entering Charing Cross railway station. The Embankment was constructed 1863–70 over the Thames mudflats both to create further space for building and transport, and to cure the stench which had haunted Londoners for many years.

ROYAL FESTIVAL HALL

The Royal Festival Hall (1951) with the Shell building (1962) beyond. The Hall and the adjacent National Film Theatre form the core of the South Bank arts complex. They were built for the Festival of Britain, held beside the Thames a century after London's Great Exhibition, as an antidote to post-war austerity.

NATIONAL THEATRE

Sir Denys Lasdun's uncompromising concrete design of the National Theatre on the South Bank (1976) has attracted admirers and detractors in equal numbers. Lasdun said, 'It's going to weather. It's going to streak. It isn't only stone that streaks … I want the concrete to weather so that in the end lichen grows on it and it becomes part of the riverscape.'

FROM WATERLOO BRIDGE

As long as I gaze on Waterloo sunset,
I am in paradise.

RAY DAVIES OF THE KINKS
Waterloo Sunset

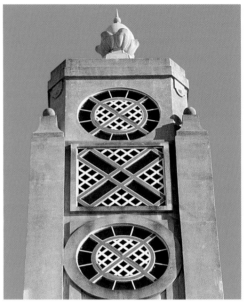

BLACKFRIARS BRIDGE

The 'pulpits' of Blackfriars Bridge remind us that for 250 years Benedictine monks (known as 'black friars' for the black habits they wore) inhabited a monastery nearby. In 1869 Queen Victoria emerged from her long period of mourning to open the bridge and was loudly hissed for doing so.

OXO TOWER

Oxo Tower Wharf, a vibrant centre for the arts housing up-market bars and brasseries, was built in the 1930s as a plant to process and store the famous stock cubes. The art deco glazing was a ruse on the part of the architect A.W. Moore to advertise the product without breaching planning regulations.

TATE MODERN

The turbine hall of the former Bankside Power Station is now the breathtakingly cavernous heart of Tate Modern, home to the Tate Gallery's collection of contemporary art. The gallery is one of the millennium developments, receiving vast numbers of visitors every year.

BLACKFRIARS RAILWAY BRIDGE

Forget six counties overhung with smoke,
Forget the snorting steam and piston stroke,
Forget the spreading of the hideous town,
Think rather of the packhorse of the down,
And dream of London, small and white and clean,
The clear Thames bordered by its gardens green.

WILLIAM MORRIS
An Earthly Paradise

MILLENNIUM BRIDGE

The Millennium Bridge, designed by Richard Rogers, links the Tate Modern at Bankside with St Paul's Cathedral. In medieval times, the north bank (visible here) eastwards to London Bridge was the centre of the medieval port, a mass of tiny wharves and commercial premises teeming with activity.

ST PAUL'S CATHEDRAL

In building a new St Paul's Cathedral after the Great Fire of 1666, Sir Christopher Wren had a constant battle with the cathedral authorities, who wanted a spire, considering a dome too Roman in style. So Wren kept his dome shrouded in scaffolding until it was far too late to change. Today the crowning glory of St Paul's is a treasured feature of London's skyline. Visitors to the cathedral with enough stamina to climb the stairs to the dome's outer balconies are rewarded with superb views over the city.

GLOBE THEATRE

Shakespeare's Globe is a faithful and atmospheric reconstruction of the 1599 theatre built a short distance away by the playwright's company, The Lord Chamberlain's Men. The original, rebuilt after being destroyed by fire in 1614, was closed by Puritans in 1642. Here visitors can savour the authentic atmosphere of plays performed as the Bard himself would have witnessed and acted in.

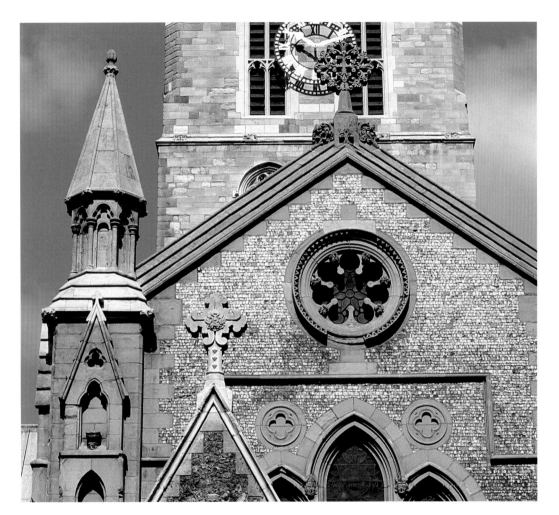

SOUTHWARK CATHEDRAL

Southwark Cathedral is a hidden jewel, somewhat oppressed by the tall buildings and railway arches that surround it. It was founded as an Augustinian church, St Mary Overie, in 1106 and rebuilt in 1212 after a fire. The chancel is a fine example of the Early English Gothic style. The nave was rebuilt in the years before 1905 when the church became a cathedral.

HAY'S GALLERIA

Hay's Galleria is a dramatic complex of upmarket shops, bars and restaurants built where once a small dock inlet penetrated the towering Victorian warehouses of Hay's Wharf. In former times this was where much of London's food and drink was unloaded and stored.

CITY HALL

City Hall, designed by Norman Foster, is the administrative building for the Greater London Authority. It is a 'green' building which uses 25 per cent of the energy used by similar-sized conventional offices. For example, it is air conditioned not by refrigeration, but by the use of cool ground water from boreholes below.

THE TOWER OF LONDON

A delight for today's visitor, the Tower of London was a place of sadness for many. In 1533 Ann Boleyn, second wife of Henry VIII, came to the Tower by barge from Greenwich for her coronation. Three years later she made the same journey, to her execution on Tower Green. The Crown Jewels are displayed here, guarded by the Tower's famous Yeoman Warders.

TOWER BRIDGE

The last of London's major river crossings to be built, Tower Bridge (1894) opens around 500 times a year to admit ships to the Pool of London. Apparently, in 1954, a bus driver to his dismay found the bridge rising to open as he drove onto it. Bravely accelerating, he managed to leap a 3-foot (1-metre) gap to land shaken but safe on the other side!

THE CIRCLE
SHAD THAMES

Shad Thames near Tower Bridge is a maze of former warehouses, linked by high-level walkways. Only a relatively few years ago these were abandoned and considered almost worthless. Now they are prestige apartments commanding huge prices.

CANARY WHARF

The huge Docklands commercial and residential development occupies the site of the former West India Docks (closed 1980) which once cut a swathe through the Isle of Dogs, a peninsula created by a loop in the Thames, once a unique and distinctive maritime community.

CANARY WHARF

Centrepiece of the Canary Wharf complex
is the 800-foot (244-metre) tower
designed by Cesar Pelli.

CANADA SQUARE

Equally important to the success of the
Docklands development has been the
Docklands Light Railway, a snaking artery
linking the City to the new commercial
centre. Here Pelli's tower is seen through the
elegant roof of Canada Square station.

MUSEUM IN DOCKLANDS

Former warehouses have now become The Museum in Docklands. 'When someone said North Quay you thought of sugar, when somebody said South Quay you thought of dates or copper … or tea.'

Bill Reegan, a former dock worker, from GAVIN WEIGHTMAN's *London River*

GREENWICH TUNNEL

The pedestrian tunnel between Greenwich and the Isle of Dogs. The world's first underwater tunnel, linking Wapping and Rotherhithe, was built between 1824 and 1842 by Marc Brunel, assisted by his son, Isambard Kingdom Brunel. Repeated flooding of the workings caused huge delay, and on one occasion, nearly cost young Brunel his life, when he was swept along the tunnel by a tide of Thames water. The reader ought to be informed that users of the Greenwich Tunnel are not allowed to whistle, carry loaded firearms or ride a tricycle.

CUTTY SARK
GREENWICH

The *Cutty Sark* originally brought tea from China, but it was on the wool run from Australia that the clipper made her name, regularly covering the 13,500 miles (22,000 km) back to England in under 80 days, the fastest-ever voyages by a sailing ship. Since 1954 she has been preserved for posterity at Greenwich.

THE OLD ROYAL NAVAL COLLEGE, Greenwich

The elegant Wren buildings which now house the University of Greenwich and the Trinity College of Music stand on the site of Placentia, a Tudor palace, where Henry VII and Henry VIII frequently stayed. Rebuilt in the 17th century (in two halves to preserve the view of Queen's House from the river), it became a naval hospital for pensioners and disabled seamen, and later, from 1873 to 1998, the Old Royal Naval College. The Great Hall has a stunning painted ceiling which took Sir James Thornhill 18 years to create.

Old Royal Naval College Chapel

OLD ROYAL NAVAL COLLEGE
GREENWICH

Perhaps no funeral in British history matched that of Admiral Lord Nelson. Killed at the moment of victory at Trafalgar, the admiral was brought back by sea to Greenwich. After lying in state in the Painted Hall of the Royal Naval College, his body was carried in state by King Charles II's royal barge to St Paul's Cathedral amid vast scenes of mourning.

QUEEN'S HOUSE
GREENWICH PARK

Greenwich Park was laid out
for Charles II, and some traces
of the original formal gardens
remain. Queen's House at the
bottom of the hill was begun
in 1616 by Inigo Jones for
Queen Anne of Denmark, and
was completed 1629–35 for
Queen Henrietta Maria. It is
now part of the National
Maritime Museum. The
museum has many strikingly
displayed delights and
discoveries from the rich
history of our seafaring nation.

OLD ROYAL OBSERVATORY, Greenwich

The Old Royal Observatory was built by Sir Christopher Wren for John Flamsteed, the first Astronomer Royal. Here the meridian line marks zero degrees, the reference point for longitude on world maps. Greenwich is also the world's reference point for time, and the red 'time ball', in 1833 the world's first public time signal, still operates.

MILLENNIUM DOME

'It was a quiet day at the Dome today, but a noisy one in Westminster'.

Nick Higham, BBC Correspondent, 2000

The Millennium Dome and the costly festivities within it attracted much criticism from politicians and others, but this striking and revolutionary building has already established itself as a dramatic landmark on the Greenwich horizon.

THAMES BARRIER

The Thames Barrier was opened in 1984 to protect the centre of London from the flooding that might occur if three factors combine: storms in the North Sea, an abnormally high tide and an east wind. An article in *The Times* once described the Barrier as 'a row of drowned Sydney Opera Houses'.

DARTFORD BRIDGE

The Queen Elizabeth II Bridge at Dartford (1991) is the last bridge on the Thames. It carries southbound traffic on the M25 high over the river and complements the two Dartford Tunnels (1963 and 1980) which handle northbound vehicles.

TILBURY FORT

'If [the ship] still ventures to go on, by which he gives them to understand he intends to run for it; then the gunner fires again, and that shot is a signal to the fortress over the river (viz.) Tilbury Fort and they immediately let fly at the ship from the guns of the east bastion and after from all the guns they can bring to bear on her.'

DANIEL DEFOE
'Customs at Gravesend' from
Tour Through England and Wales

TILBURY POWER STATION

'Essex, when you get beyond the immediate influence of the gorgings and disgorgings of the Wen [London], that is to say, beyond the demand for crude vegetables and repayment in manure, is by no means a fertile county.'

WILLIAM COBBETT
Rural Rides

THE CHURCH OF ST HELEN
CLIFFE, KENT

'The King to the Sheriff of Kent, greeting. Because we have been given to understand that a great mass of whale lately cast ashore by the coast of the River Thames ... in your county ... and whereof a great part has been carried away by evildoers in contempt of us ... we order you ... that you cause all the whale aforesaid to be entirely delivered without any delay to our beloved and trusty Nicholas de la Beche, constable of our Tower of London.'

The Fine Roll of Edward III, 1337

… I'd have you know that these waters of mine
Were once a branch of the River Rhine,
When hundreds of miles to the East I went
And England was joined to the Continent.

RUDYARD KIPLING
The River's Tale

near CLIFFE
Kent

On the salt marshes of north Kent, the Thames recaptures the tranquillity of its upper reaches. The lonely skeletons of sailing boats are a poignant reminder that the open sea is but a few miles away.

HADLEIGH CASTLE

Hadleigh Castle, once one of the most important fortifications in Essex, overlooks from a height the Thames as it broadens towards the far coast of Kent. It was famously painted by John Constable. In the distance is the oil storage terminal at Canvey Island.

LEIGH-ON-SEA

The last few miles of the Thames shoreline are all built-up areas. Leigh-on-Sea, once an isolated fishing village on the Essex marshes, still retains some of its ancient charm.

SOUTHEND-ON-SEA

Southend-on-Sea is the traditional playground of London's East Enders. Packed paddle steamers once carried day trippers from London Bridge, and even today three million visitors arrive each year, perhaps to walk on the pier, at $1^1/_4$ miles (2 km) thought to be the longest in the world, to brave the rides at the famous Kursaal pleasure beach, to shop or just to browse the pubs and arcades on 'the Golden Mile'.

[The Thames] … is the privileged place for fish and ships, the glory and wealth of the city, the highway to the sea, the bringer-in of wealth and strangers, and his business is all for water, yet he deals much with the land too: he is a little sea, and a great river.

Donald Lupton
London and the Country Carbonadoed

Sunset over Leigh-on-Sea from Southend Pier

Select Bibliography

Cobbett, William: *Rural Rides*, first published 1830

Davies, Gareth Huw: *A Walk Along the Thames Path*, Michael Joseph, 1989

Grahame, Kenneth: *The Wind in the Willows*, Egmont Books, first published 1908

Jenkins, Alan & Brabbs, D.: *The Book of the Thames*, Macmillan/Book Club Associates, 1983

Jerome, Jerome K.: *Three Men in a Boat*, first published 1889

Martin, Frank: *History, People and Places in the Thames Valley*, Spurbooks, 1972

Massingham, Hugh & Pauline: *The London Anthology*, Spring Books

Mitchell, R.J. & Leys, M.D.R.: *A History of London Life*, Longmans/Pelican, 1963

Mortimer, John D.: *An Anthology of the Home Counties*, Methuen, 1947

Tames, Richard: *A Traveller's History of London*, Windrush Press, 1992

Weightman, Gavin: *London River*, Collins & Brown, 1990

Insight Guide to London, APA Publications

Nicholson *Ordnance Survey Guide to the River Thames*, OS and Collins

The website 'River Thames and Boaty Things' is a delightful compendium of information about the Thames. It can be found at http://dhart.future.easyspace.com/thames.htm.

Doorway of thatched cottage, Clifton Hampden, Oxon

The gardens at Buscot House, Oxfordshire

Index

Pagoda, Kew Gardens

GROUNDCOVER
SERIES